CW01073127

www.booksbyboxer.com

No part of this publication may be reproduced or transmitted in any form or by any means, electronic or mechanical, including photocopying, recording or any information storage and retrieval system, or for the source of ideas without written permission from the publisher.

Bee Three Publishing is an imprint of Books By Boxer
Published by
Books By Boxer, Leeds, LS13 4BS, UK
Books by Boxer (EU), Dublin, D02 P593, IRELAND
Boxer Gifts LLC, 955 Sawtooth Oak Cir, VA 22802, USA
© Books By Boxer 2024
All Rights Reserved
MADE IN CHINA
ISBN: 9781915410740

This book is produced from responsibly sourced paper to ensure forest management

All Rights Reserved by Ann Edwards Art ©

SOME PEOPLE AGE
LIKE **WINE**, SOME
PEOPLE AGE LIKE
CHEESE...

EITHER WAY IT'S
A **WIN**.

GIN IS EVEN **MORE**
NUTRITIOUS THE
<u>OLDER</u> YOU ARE!

YOU KNOW
YOU'RE GETTING
OLD WHEN THE
CANDLES **COST**
MORE THAN THE
CAKE...

AND YOU HAVE TO
WARN THE **FIRE
DEPARTMENT** AS A
PRECAUTION.

AN OLD DOG **CAN**
LEARN NEW
TRICKS.

IF THEY'RE
SIMPLE.

YOUR COLORS STILL
SHINE BRIGHT...

EVEN THOUGH
YOU'VE GONE
GRAY !

YOU STILL LOOK
CLUCKIN' GREAT!

THIS ISN'T GRAY, IT'S *SILVER AND FOXY!*

STAYING IN...

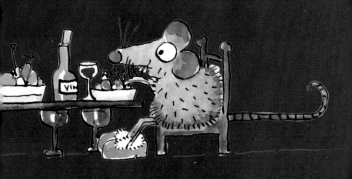

IS THE NEW
GOING OUT.

EVEN THOUGH
YOU'RE **OLD**...

YOU CAN STILL DRINK LIKE A *FISH!*

EXCEPT WHEN
IT COMES TO
PASSWORDS,
BIRTHDAYS, WHERE
THEIR GLASSES
ARE...

I FOLD...

I'M OLD...

A CLEVER OLD TROUT.

YOU'RE **NEVER** TOO OLD TO PARTY...

EVEN IF YOU GO
HOME *EARLY* !

CAN WE NOT MENTION MY MENTION MY GRAYING ROOTS?

OLD AGE IS ALL
ABOUT *BALANCE*...

HOW EARLY IS **TOO EARLY** TO GO TO BED ?

THERE'S STILL **LIFE** IN THE OLD BIRD YET...

BUT PARENTING *REALLY* TAKES IT OUT OF YOU!

YOU'RE STILL A
CATCH!

ONCE A QUEEN BEE, **ALWAYS A** QUEEN BEE.

AGE HASN'T
CHANGED YOU...

YOU'RE STILL **_WEIRD_**!

NOW YOU HAVE ALL THE TIME IN THE WORLD...

*TO BECOME
A CROSSWORD
CHAMPION !*

YOU'VE **STILL** GOT IT !

IT WOULD BE RUDE
TO CALL YOU A
DAFT OLD BAT...

BUT THERE ARE
TIMES IT SEEMS
APPROPRIATE.

KNITTING ROCKS
AND CROCHET
ROLLS!

YOU'VE SLOWED DOWN A BIT...

BUT AT LEAST YOU
HAVEN'T STOPPED!

WITH **AGE** COMES **WISDOM**, SO... WHICH ONE CAME FIRST?

KEEP **FLAPPING**
YOUR WINGS...

OR YOU'LL **FALL**
OUT OF THE SKY !

AS YOU GET **OLDER,** DO TRY TO KEEP UP...

YOUR *SPORTING*
ENDEAVOURS !

REMEMBER TO
KEEP UP WITH YOUR
BEAUTY SLEEP!

THESE ARE **NOT** WRINKLES, I JUST **CREASED** IN MY SLEEP!

YOU'RE STILL
AS MAD AS THE
MARCH HARE!

THERE'S *STILL LIFE*
IN THE OLD DOG
YET !

YOU MIGHT BE
ABLE TO DRINK
LIKE YOU'RE
YOUNGER...

BUT YOU WILL STILL **FEEL OLD IN THE** MORNING !

THE **OLDER** AND MORE **FORGETFUL** YOU GET...

YOUR **OLD** FRIENDS
BECOME YOUR
NEW FRIENDS !

TRY TO **REMEMBER**
WHERE YOU HID
YOUR NUTS!

OLDER...
BUT **DEFINITELY**
NOT WISER!

EWE STILL HAVE TIME TO TRY NEW THINGS !

DANCE LIKE NOBODY IS WATCHING...

BUT PERHAPS
CLOSE THE
CURTAINS.

YOU CAN STILL
DRINK TO
EXTINCTION !

FOR THE LAST TIME... YOUR GLASSES ARE ON YOUR HEAD!

HOW *MERLOT* CAN *YOU GO?!*

DO YOU
REMEMBER WHEN
SURFING DIDN'T
MEAN *THIS*?

DON'T UNDERESTIMATE

AN *OLD GUY* ON A
BICYCLE !

SLOW AND STEADY
WINS THE RACE...

NOW IS THE PERFECT TIME...

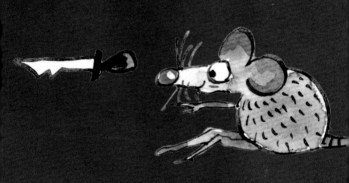

TO TAKE UP NEW
HOBBIES.

TAKE IT **EASY**...

YOU'VE EARNT IT.

AT A CERTAIN AGE,
LADIES BECOME
MORE INTERESTED
IN **TALKING FROGS**
THAN PRINCES...

WHO ARE YOU CALLING A DINOSAUR?

IT'S ALL DOWNHILL FROM HERE...

SO *ENJOY* THE RIDE!